Perfect Blend

Helping Stepfamilies Thrive

by

Oscar & Crystal Jones

DEDICATION

We dedicate this book to all blended families all over the earth. Families can come together as one and thrive, no matter what the blend. The caveat is to submit them to God first. Let all that you do be for His glory alone.

CONTENTS

ACKNOWLEDGMENTS

We acknowledge our Faithful Father who has guided us in successfully navigating our family relationships. We thank Him for His grace to write this book and His lavish love that He continually bestows upon us.

We are thankful to our son, Pastor Jake Allen who is the apple of our eye, our first born son with promise. We appreciate your contribution to this book. And your contribution to our family. You are a tremendous blessing to all of us.

Thank you to our other four children, Kyria, Charity, LaTina, and Christopher. You, too, were a part of the blending process. Each of you treated Jake the same as you treated each other. (That wasn't always good, but it was best).

Thank you Aries Winans who worked hard on the cover design to help us get this book out in a timely fashion.

Finally, we would like to acknowledge Martha Jean Allen who has gone on to be with the Lord. God brought Jake to us through her. She was a beautiful example of God's grace. We love her and miss her.

1
PERFECT?

Why would we title this book on blended families as Perfect Blend? We do not intend to convey that there is a perfect formula to blending families. According to Merriam Webster, the word 'perfect' has several meanings. But we want to highlight two:

Per`fect: adjective

1a: being entirely without fault or defect: FLAWLESS.

2b: lacking in no essential detail: COMPLETE

We do not chose the definition that asserts to be without fault or flawless. There is no such family on the earth. The first family, Adam and Eve were blemished even though they had no natural parents; but the perfect parent, God Himself. And still their family was dysfunctional. Their eldest son was consumed with jealousy and killed his younger brother. This was the tragic result of sin entering the earth. So there is no family that is perfected, step or biological. We don't want to give the illusion that a perfect family is even a thing. That's not our aim.

When we use the word 'perfect', we refer to a state of being complete. We want families to be healthy and whole. That means the family will have all the necessary tools for growth. We want to help them cover all of the bases, leaving no part of their family unit at risk. It is our aim to help stepfamilies grow and thrive, to be well-rounded and bring glory and honor to God. The goal is to learn how to overcome the hurdles and complications that present themselves -not to avoid them or ignore them; and to keep love at the base.

Our God is able to bring beauty out of ashes. It's not *what* we offer Him that matters. The point is to offer Him whatever we have, totally trusting Him to make it better. He makes all things beautiful in His time.

Blending families successfully takes commitment, patience, and faith in God. There is no guarantee that the process will be without impediments or tears. In fact, the opposite is probably more true. There will be difficulties, trouble, and quarrels. Perfect blending means we will have to press through the 'stuff' to get to oneness. We won't abort or short circuit the process. But we will finish. We will complete what we said we would do.

It is important to understand from the onset that blending a family can be overwhelming, but it is imperative that we keep at it. If you are going to be in it for the long haul, you will have to take some time for yourself. Breathe. Take a walk. Soak in a bath. Drink something hot. Get a massage. Exercise. There will be many days that you will need to get your head in the right space. Don't feel guilty about it. It's healthy to administer self-care so that you can better care for those that you love. That's part of blending in a 'perfect' or complete way. Do whatever is necessary to blow off steam so that it is not directed at your family. And allow your spouse some self-care as well. Sometimes, you may even need to get away together. It's okay. You aren't failing. This is a sign that you are winning.

On the other side of overwhelming is something spectacular that will bless our God. So take those breaks. Take them often but get back in the game.

Our family is blended. It has not been without lumps. Our son has been an extraordinary blessing in our lives.

Our blending started when he was about 2 years old. Today he is an exemplary man of God. He contributed his story to this book. He writes the next chapter from his perspective. We wanted you to see all sides of our story. May this book bless you and give you wisdom for your own journey. We pray that your own family is a wonderful example of God's grace.

2
FIRST BORN

Being considered "half" in a family is discomforting to anyone, especially a child. It is a feeling of illegitimacy. As I revisited the feelings and emotions that came with this new form of living (having two mothers, two dads, half-brothers and half-sisters), it did not feel good. Being 'half' in a family makes a person feel a little 'less than'. I am so grateful to have being made whole in Christ Jesus.

Life for a step-child can be hurtful. But fortunately for me I never really had to live with such a demeaning title or position. There were no prefixes added to my position in the family. I wasn't referred to as a stepson or half-brother. However, it still did a number on me that my parents were not married to each other.

Throughout my young adult years, I would constantly compare my step-parents; particularly my step-mom to my biological mom. My mom was the standard and my step-mom could never measure up. Though my step-mom had an unconditional love for me, my love for her was very conditional. I drew clear and defined lines about where she was welcomed in my life. I often saw her as a threat to being a replacement in my heart for my biological mom. The way she communicated love for me felt very different. This was mainly because their personalities were very different. Subsequently, I felt challenged to choose one over the other rather than accepting them both as mom. As a child, I was too immature to understand that I could have the best of both of these worlds.

This lead to a lot of rough patches emotionally and spiritually for me. It was emotionally rough because I would often cry as a child whenever I had to visit my dad for the summer and be around my step-mom. I thought she was too different from who my biological mom was. Because of that, I didn't accept her love for me. And whenever I talked to my mom, I felt pulled in both directions. It was spiritually rough because I felt it was God's fault that my life was so divided. I wanted what every other child wants... for both of my parents to be together. And I just didn't understand why God wouldn't give that to me.

While still coming to grips with living life with two moms, my biological mom decided to get married. This was a devastating blow to an already bruised heart. I had not yet figured "it" out with my stepmom; and my mom was adding a step-dad to my equation. I was upset, to say the least. I was such a momma's boy. I thought I was being replaced in my mother's heart by another man. This caused me to struggle with my self-image and my place in the family. I was deeply wounded.

I, literally, cried at my mom's wedding and was purposely uninvolved because of the resentment and bitterness I had toward my mom's husband, even though he never did anything to or against me. To others, I made him out to be a monster. None of it was true. He loved my mom and cared for her so deeply. But as a child, I needed affirmation. Unfortunately the adults in my life were not tuned in to what I needed. So I festered in my rejection. When children feel rejection, they reject or push back.

Having a step-dad was slightly different for me, because he and I were not as communicative as I was with my step-mom. I treated him slightly better than my step-mom because he was a lot less hands on. That was the way I preferred to be parented – hands off. My dad's wife aka my other mom was hands on and heart fully in. My response was to push her away by treating her harshly.

Being a step-child can be difficult if proper communication is not made to allow the feelings and emotions of the child to be addressed.

The worst part of being a step-child was the feeling that I wasn't being genuinely and completely loved like the biological children were. I believed my step-parents were taking my place and interfering with my relationships with my biological parents. In my mind, it contributed to me receiving less (gifts and financial support) and experiencing less of the presence of my biological parents. The addition of these extra people, subtracted from me. Life would've been better if they were not in the picture. I also assigned blame to my stepparents as the reason my biological parents were not together. I often would harbor deep resentment and anger toward my stepparents even if they did nothing to me. I thought evil and so I behaved evil.

Once I grew in my relationship with God, I began to allow that part of my heart to go through the healing process. I then began to hold myself accountable for my actions. My thought patterns began to change. I was open with my feelings and more receptive of constructive criticism. It took a prayer on my behalf to allow the Lord to put my step-mom in my heart like He did for her. Prior to my relationship with God I didn't want her in my heart, as if she had given birth to me. I had moments of deep brokenness before God to accept my step-mom into her rightful position in my heart. She was 'step' to me even though I was not 'step' to her. God showed me that I was only a stepchild or 'half' child in my own eyes. This was one of the greatest revelations of my life. God certainly never viewed me as a 'half' or 'step'; and my mom didn't either. It was all in my head.

As I began to heal, I saw that there were so many benefits to having her as my stepmom. I was actually limiting my progression in life because I wouldn't receive her wise counsel.

One of the greatest gifts I received from God was two mothers in this earth. What the enemy meant for evil, God turned it all around for my good.

Unfortunately, my biological mom has gone on to be with the Lord. But God in his entire splendor privileged me to have another mother that cares for me as deeply as my biological mom did. It has been one of my greatest regrets that I did not love her (in the early years) the way she (my step-mom) loved me. I am sure I caused her much pain and hurt because of how I treated her. Nevertheless she never retaliated against me or mistreated me in any way. She waited patiently on me to get it. And I did. It took years, but I did get it. Blood alone does not determine family. Jesus was the stepson of Joseph, but throughout scripture he was referred to as the son of Joseph and the son of the carpenter. If we indicate that someone is my step____ (fill in the blank), we are essentially saying to the world, they aren't my blood. Blending works best when we can drop the 'step' and just be family.

3
STEPPING IN

When we first were married, I, Crystal, asked the Lord to put Jake (my husband's 2 year old baby boy) in my heart as if I had given birth to him. I didn't want to be the wicked stepmother of fairytales or even real-life tales. Nor did I want to be distant and indifferent. I look back on that time and think, "What a odd request from a 20 year old!" The thing about such a weighty petition is that it couldn't have originated from such a young, simple heart. It is God who put that desire within me. The scripture says that it is He that works in us the will and do of his good pleasure. So I can take no credit for any part of it. God initiates the passion and then He fills it.

Even though I was not a mother at the time, God was stirring motherhood inside of me. My firstborn would be this son that God had gifted me. I wanted to mother Jake as I would mother my future children. I wanted there to be no difference between he and his siblings. I wanted him to feel love, acceptance and trust. I most certainly did not want him to experience the rejection that often comes with blended families. And even though I prayed the prayer, the answer did not come overnight. It would be our journey. We would get there, but not without a mound of hurdles to overcome.

But there is something you should know. I, too, am a stepchild. Early in my life, my parents divorced. My dad was the first to remarry. I felt so rejected and lost. My dad had an entire new family. I didn't feel like I was a part of it. I remember struggling to know and accept myself. I changed the spelling of my first name so many times that it is misspelled on my high school diploma. I also toyed with different last names, too. I even asked my mom to change it, legally. She refused. Thank God for that.

Rejection attached itself to me and I carried it throughout my childhood and young adult life. For many years, I felt my stepmom didn't like me. As I matured, I understood it wasn't her. There were a lot of dynamics that played into my skewed perception. And none of the fault lied with her.

My step-mom has unwittingly taught me a lot about

love. I have seen her sow love into so many people who weren't connected to her by blood. She is such a generous giver and a remarkable servant. She is truly one of a kind. My stepmom is one of the most loving and selfless people I've ever known. I love her and am loved by her. She is a gift to me. But I didn't see it right away. It took some growing up on my part. I was stewing in my own rejection, but her love helped me to grow.

The enemy wants to capture our children, as early as possible. So he sends the spirit of rejection to attach itself to them. Every child who is separated from a parent experiences some type of rejection to some extent. If the child is born out of wedlock, abandoned by a parent (through divorce or separation), or if a parent marries someone else, the child will feel the weight of that loss. Even if the child stuffs his emotions or shows no sign of loss, he/she is still greatly impacted.

A new stepparent entering the broken family has to be sensitive to that. Children hurt. And they have no control over their hurt. It's massive and wild and the child wants to contain it. But they are often unsure of how to do that. The issue is not just about their parents getting back together. Even though that is often a factor. But what is most at risk is the child's identity. They often struggle with knowing who they are. What is their new role? Will they be liked by the new family? Will they be seen as disloyal if they like the new stepparent? How do they fit in with the other children? Will they be excluded or treated differently by the stepfamily? Will their biological parent reject them now that they have a new family? They have so many questions whirling around in those little heads. Often they are too afraid of the possible answers to even ask the questions.

However communication is key. Both biological parents should strive to get along as best they can for the benefit of the innocent children. Talk to them. Try to answer some of those questions in a way that eases their tensions.

It is extremely important how the new spouse enters into the family. The wise stepparent enters with sensitivity and wisdom. He or she doesn't get to come in "laying down the law" so to speak. The stepparent should be gentle, affirming and loving. Leave all discipline to the biological parent early in the relationship. It is easier on the relationship if the biological parent handles all tough decisions and correction. That doesn't mean the stepparent doesn't have any say. But he/she should not be the one to mete out the discipline.

If you want the stepchild to respect you, make sure you respect his/her feelings. Even if the child is resistant in the beginning, you can win them over by giving him/her space to grieve. If their parents divorced, grieving isn't over just because the divorce is done. It kind of goes into remission for the children, so to speak. And it resurfaces when mom or dad has a new love interest. Even if the parents were never married and decided to marry someone else later in life, it's the same effect for the child. Change in family dynamics will cause the pain to come alive. An aggressive stepparent can make things worse. If you are the stepparent, you should walk lightly. Talk to God and your spouse about your role.

The stepparent should come into the family offering compassion and understanding, leaving room for the child to adjust. Never force the child to accept the new stepparent. Give the child space and time. Certainly draw clear boundaries about respect and manners. The child needs to understand that disrespect will not be tolerated. This includes talking back, carrying an attitude, engaging in the silent treatment, and yelling at the stepparent. The biological parent needs to establish and maintain those clear boundaries. And set repercussions for if/when the child crosses the line.

However allow the child to work through his/her emotions. It would help if the child could talk about his emotions in a nonjudgmental environment. It would be good to have family meetings once a week. Allow children to express their feelings, both positive and negative. And then solicit the child's input on how to make things better.

Both spouses will need to sit down and discuss your own parenting styles. So you will know how to handle situations before they occur. What you believe about discipline and chores needs to be clearly communicated. Discuss and decide how you will move forward. Never assume that these things are obvious because they are not. Even parents without the "step" dynamic may find that they differ in parenting styles. An agreement must be reached or you could give the child mixed signals.

A wife can't decide to parent her children one way and her husband's children another. You must be consistent. Operate as a cohesive unit. If the situation arises where you have to referee a quarrel between stepsiblings, the best course of action may to simply be a good listener. Ask all involved for their side, and listen carefully. Avoid showing favoritism and giving one-size-fits-all punishments. If the two of you need to take time to pray to see how you will address it, do so.

The stepparent has to be intentional that he/she does not favor their biological child or the stepchild when discrepancies arise. There is a natural tendency to feel protective toward your own child, or you might feel like you want to "win over" your spouse's child. But either position is unhealthy. You should not parent out of distrust or guilt. This could create a bigger wedge in your family.

Some stepparents try to come in buying the child's love. This is extremely unhealthy. Gift-giving will seal your position 'outside' of the family. Kids will see right through you and often try to manipulate you for more bounty. A real parent doesn't buy their way in. *They love their way in.*

The biological parents will do well to help the child understand who she is and is not. Let him/her know:

She is not just floating in the abyss without a family or family structure.

- You are her family, custodial or not. You will always be her dad or mom.
- Let her know that you will always be an important part of each other's lives.
- There is purpose for her and she is loved.

Children and teens need to hear it even if you think they are not responding to it. Tell them anyway. You must hammer at that spirit of rejection head on.

It is unreasonable to come into a new family expecting to have the same type of interactions that you share with you own biological children. It takes time to build. It is important that you allow time for your new family to blend and take on its own identity. It may be very different from what you have built with your own biological children and that is okay.

Children have a lot to process. Your children may be dealing with two sets of parents and two sets of rules. In that case, they will need lots of grace.

Be mindful that your noncustodial child is not treated like a visitor when spending time with the family. Certain places shouldn't be off limits. Make sure he/she has a place (container) for their toiletries and other items inside of the home. They shouldn't have to tote a toothbrush every single time they come to their other parent's home.

A stepparent isn't a replacement parent, even if that parent is absent or deceased. I wasn't there to replace Jake's mother, Martha. God doesn't replace people. He adds and multiplies to our lives. I was there to be a blessing to Oscar and Martha and this beautiful baby boy with whom they had been blessed. I was allowed an important place and privilege to come alongside of them in this calling to raise him.

The stepparent has to do the heart work to avoid feelings of rejection and inadequacy. Blending becomes difficult if the stepparent takes personally any of the stuff that the kids throw their way. Some of the jabs will be intentional. But know when that happens, the child is uncomfortable and trying to find their place in the family. That doesn't mean you overlook bad behavior. On the contrary, it must be dealt with by the biological parent. However, you just can't take it to heart. Keep praying. Keep loving and keep trying. You have to remember step-parenting is certainly not for the faint of heart.

To be honest I, Oscar, didn't think about blending a family when I first married my wife. I was newly married and in love with my wife and was excited to start a life with her. I loved my son tremendously and spent lots of time with him. I wanted my son and I wanted my wife. I really didn't think about how it would all work out. As many people do, I just assumed that my wife would accept my son and my son would accept my wife. That's not an assumption any one should make. I just took life as it came. There were no books read, no preparation made at all. I was young and naive.

I didn't know about the prayer that my wife had prayed in those early days. Looking back at it, I can see the love she had for God. We both stepped into this life together as babies ourselves; and neither of us had the first clue about parenting or all that it would entail.

Learning how to navigate your role as a parent can be challenging. And it can be especially difficult for a stepparent.

I had to balance the relationship between my wife, my son, and my son's mother. This is a delicate balancing act that must be undergirded with much prayer and thoughtfulness. This works best when everyone is on the same team.

It would've been a disaster if my wife and I had not

been on the same team. I would have been pulled in all directions. I am thankful for a wife who wanted to please God. She made it easier for me. She was supportive and encouraged my relationship with my son. She also sought to build her own relationship with my son's mother. This was a great blessing.

The adults in the life of these children should pray and ask God for wisdom and guidance to do what is in their best interest. Stepparents should petition the Lord to put that child in your heart as if her/she were your own. And act on it by faith.

This is not easy nor a quick-fix. It is definitely a spiritual matter and the will of God. It can't be done just by praying the prayer. That's only the first step. You must really have a desire to affectionately love that child. But it can be done, as it has been done by my wife and many others. **Ask the Holy Spirit to help pave the way. Because the road can be quite bumpy. And be patient. It takes time for a family to blend.**

OSCAR & CRYSTAL JONES

4
TUG OF WAR

When we went as a married couple, to pick up Jake for the first time from his Mom, it was difficult. He was just a baby and he screamed and kicked and clenched to his mom's clothes as tight as those tiny little hands could. His eyes were pleading with her to not let him go with these strangers. She handed him over to us, turned quickly and ran into the house with tears slowly streaming down her face. I'd never seen a mother so strong. She chose what was in the best interest of her child even though it hurt her heart.

Martha was an amazing woman. She never withheld Jake from us. We had complete and total access to him. She didn't parent out of spite. She encouraged the relationship with his dad and his new wife from day one. It was difficult for her. But it was necessary for her son.

It is never good to force a child to choose between his parents. Most people get both a mom and a dad in their lives, but some children are only allowed one or the other. This is sad for the child. It is understandable if one is deceased or dangerous. But some parents do not allow access to the other parent or they only allow limited access because of their own toxicity. These restrictions usually harm the child more than anyone else.

The toxic parent speaks negatively about the other parent to the child or in front of the child. In such cases the child is discouraged to think or speak well of the 'other' parent. He/she knows there is an unspoken rule in their house, "You can't like daddy or his new family. It would harm Mom, too much." And so the child has to fight to stay bitter or stuff their true feelings for the sake of the other parent. That's hard on a little person and emotionally exhausting. When both parents fight, children know it and feel it. It's tough on them. They want to be *normal* and be able to love both parents without repercussions.

A child with two homes should be encouraged to embrace both families. He will need both his mother and his father, equally. It's the way God designed it. Whatever fallout there is from the parents' previous relationships, it belongs to the adults. The children should not be made to suffer for the mistakes of their parents.

Avoid competition for the child's affection. A child's love for his mother is separate from his love for his father. Humans are created with a huge capacity to love. So when a child loves a noncustodial parent, it is not an indictment on the custodial parent. And the parent should not feel threatened. It actually demonstrates healthy parenting. Parents have to be secure within themselves to produce secure children. No parent has to diminish the other to make themselves feel better. A healthy parent does not speak ill or infer ill against the noncustodial parent.

Sometimes couples are spurred into a custody battle. Preoccupation with how to make ends meet and how to navigate the turbulent times ahead can cause parents to lose focus. Parents can get so locked in on the war that they really lose sight of the child and the damage that is being caused to him/her. More time and attention is given to the case than to the little humans at the center of it. If you find yourself in this situation, be intentional about affirming your child. Don't make the fight more important than the child. Be sensitive and wise.

Jake never *had* to choose between loving his mom and loving his dad. We operated as a team even though we didn't always agree. I, Crystal, was included in meetings about what would happen in Jake's life, because it was necessary. I was completely involved in his care. Not only that, our whole family would be affected by these decisions. There were many times that Jake's mother, Martha and I had discussions without my husband present. I would fill my husband in later. We were two moms coming in agreement for what was best for "our" son. My husband and Jake's mom both trusted me. Don't misunderstand, it didn't start out this way. We had to build to this place. I had to be patient and use wisdom.

Because I didn't overstep my bounds, I was invited in. Martha welcomed me as part of Jake's village. If blending is going to be successful, the parents and step-parents will have to be on the same page. Everyone needs to be on the same team, operating from the same play book.

What good does it do anyone if you are at odds with each other? The adults have to be mature enough to communicate properly. It is only a problem when the adults act like children, bickering and arguing and fighting for control.

Your child has a village and if his/her village is at war with each other, how can the child win? He will surely suffer. Be as cooperative as you possibly can. Be on board and present. Even if one parent is toxic, keep aiming to make it work for the benefit of the child. Follow peace with all men as much it lies within you (Romans 12:18).

It's amazing how much good a simple conversation can do. Spend time praying. Then both parents should discuss together how to discipline, chores, bedtimes, homework, etc. Communicate regarding all relevant information. Work to come to a place of agreement. If you don't agree, give valid reasons. But be willing to concede to make things better for your child. If you try something that doesn't work, don't play the "I told you so" card. It's unproductive and does not grease the wheels of cooperation. Over the life of the child, you both will make mistakes. That's just life. But do the very best you can to work together.

A custodial mother can often feel a sense of ownership when it comes to her babies. She can feel that she has more power, authority, and voice because she was the one to physically give birth. Dads often get side swiped in the process and their input is minimized. This is unfair.

Decisions should not be made by one parent if both parents are actively involved. On the other hand, a noncustodial parent can only expect to have as much input as he/she is involved. When parents cooperate in the best interest of the child everybody wins.

5
CHOSEN

Before I formed thee in the belly I knew thee; and before thou camest forth out of the womb I sanctified thee...
Jeremiah 1:5a

Our son, Jake, came into the earth because God sent him. He was born on purpose. While it may have been an accident for his parents, who had engaged in sexual sin, this young man's birth was no mistake. He had to be born. It was the intentional plan of God for Jake to come into the earth at precisely the day and hour he was born. He had a divine mandate to carry out God's assignment. And so it was, God breathed the breath of life into his tiny body. And a man child was born. God used man's sin to bring forth His chosen seed.

God certainly does not sanction or advocate sin. We know and understand that. But He can take the evil and turn it for good. Make no mistake, there are no "illegitimate" children in God's eyes.

If God has a plan for our stepchildren, who are we to reject or try to block that plan, simply because we don't like the other parent or we feel threatened by the relationship with the child and his parent? It is a dangerous thing for a stepparent to stand as an obstacle to the child and his biological parent.

On the flip side, it can be an incredible blessing when we allow God to bring us together in covenant and community as a family. It is He who sets the solitary into families. We reap some amazing rewards when God is allowed to carry out His plan. Our job is to agree with God's plan for the children entrusted to our care.

God is the orchestrator of life. It is His breath that gives each of us life. He knows us. He formed us. When we are in covenant with Him, it's His plan that governs and directs our lives.

Psalm 127:3 Lo, children are an heritage of the LORD: and the fruit of the womb is his reward. Every person born has a purpose to fulfill whether they walk in it or not. *I know the thoughts I have toward you of peace and not of evil to give you a hope and a future. Jeremiah 1:17*

We (Oscar, Martha, and I) were the team chosen to make sure Jake became all that God intended. Just as the child who draws his mother a picture with the art supplies she gives him, we offer back to God this man-child, he entrusts to us. These children (step and biological) belong to God. We are simply made stewards over their lives.

We must direct them and point them to Jesus. It's our responsibility to do all that is in our power to raise responsible adults who love God, are selfless, and contribute to their community.

It is selfish to consider 'what I want or need' instead of what's best for the child? Even though a custodial parent may *want* the child to live with him or her, he/she should consider if that is what is best for the child. When a child's needs are primary, that means we must minimize what we want; because ultimately we want what is best for our children. Parenting can't stem from – but I will miss him, or I will be lonely if he goes there. Parenting has to be about what will make my child a respectable adult who loves God and has good character.

At the end of the day, our children (step or biological), do not belong to us. God is the one who caused their lives to come forth. He is their ultimate parent. He has a plan for their lives that trumps ours. Therefore parents will do well to pray about every decision and allow God to set the outcome. Be open to His will. He is omniscient and perfect. He can be trusted.

Philippians 4:6 says Be careful for nothing; but in everything by prayer and supplication with thanksgiving let your requests be made known unto God. When you don't know what to do, God always does. Every situation you face as parents has a God-ordained wisdom for it. Our duty is to simply ask God which path to take and He will lead us. I Thessalonians 5:17 says, pray without ceasing.

On Jake's graduation day, he decided he would no longer call me Mama, but would put some distance between us by calling me by my first name. It hurt me to the core. It felt like he was twisting a dagger in my heart. It wasn't just that he was being disrespectful, even though that was a part of it. He had been raised to never address adults by their first name. We always taught our children to put a handle on it (Aunt, Uncle, Mr., Mrs., etc.). So that was bad, but what made it worse is that he was rejecting me as his mother, a role I held for nearly 16 years of his life. I went to my husband and insisted that he do something. He refused. He turned me on my heels and pushed me back to face "my son". I didn't want to because I was too hurt. The rejection was overwhelming. I took it, personally. My husband insisted, "You must be the one who deals with this. He said it to you. So, as his mother, you must correct him." I wasn't new to this. Jake and I had been in this for most of his life. My husband's reasoning made sense, even though that is not what I wanted to hear. Reluctantly, I did correct Jake and he quickly submitted himself. It became apparent that he was testing me. He was feeling himself.

He relented, but there would be much more testing in my future. I would need to guard my heart. Guarding my heart didn't mean I needed to distance myself from my son or to withhold love from him. It simply meant that I must protect my heart from offense and bitterness.

A year later, his mother sent him and his 18 month old daughter to live with us after graduation. He was 19. Martha was concerned about his behavior and the trouble to which he seemed to be attracted. He was gambling, drinking, and engaging in all types of distasteful behaviors. So she didn't ask Jake's permission. The three of us talked about it and we made the decision for him. He conceded but not with any fervor. He wanted to be with his dad but he had decided he had enough of me.

When he came to us, he rejected our lifestyle as pastors. He snubbed me as his mom. He was respectful but there was a resistance of the way we governed life. He missed his mother's side of the family. He made it a point of letting us know he was connected to them. He was an "Allen", not a "Jones". This consistent taunting would often break my husband's heart.

At some point Jake decided to make the best of it. God had a plan and his life began to change for the better. Eventually, he gave his life to the Lord. His mom sighed with relief. It was confirmation to her that she had made the right decision. Life for Jake was good.

Three years later, Martha phoned. She had some news that she wanted to share with us. She had been diagnosed with cancer. She asked us not to share it with Jake. "Why?" I asked. She explained that she didn't want him coming back to the town she lived in. It just wasn't good for him. He was doing so well with us, she reasoned. I convinced her that he had a right to know. She reluctantly agreed. The following year, she died. And just as she feared, he returned to the town and the life he had left.

With the burial of his mother came the resurfacing of the old feelings. Jake resented me with every fiber of who he was. I could see it in his eyes and feel it in his coldness. He fought me, not physically, but emotionally. He wished it was me instead of Martha who had died. He was angry at God and the world. He went back to his former life of sleeping around, drinking and drugs. He left God in utter defiance. He felt God wasn't there for his mom, so why should he be there for God. And he transferred every bit of disappointment and rage he felt upon his father's wife. He hated me.

He ran wild. He didn't understand fully what he was running from, but I did. I had dreams about him. The Lord would show me what he was doing and who he was doing it with. I would tell my husband. I would also share it with Jake. He was always astonished at the precision at which I could tell him what was going on in his life and I was over a thousand miles away. But it was God showing his love for this runaway child. His eyes were in every place, nudging his son back home.

Jake lost nearly everything in his rebellion. Some of his friends and family members turned against him. Like a momma bear robbed of her cub, I drove those 1 thousand miles to be at his defense.

Jake could not escape my love. It was too late for him. He was mine. He was locked into my heart for better and for worse. And this was the worse. But I still loved him. He was still mine. I never went back on what I asked God to do. He was in my heart as if I had given birth to him. Even though he was rejecting me, I continued to choose him.

When my husband and I married, Jake didn't get to choose me as his mother. So he really had no right to un-choose me as his mother. There was nothing he could do to make me stop loving him. Believe me, he tried. We've had many run-ins but we always recovered. Because I am his "real" mom. And real moms don't give up. Through the good, bad, and the ugly, he is our son. In my heart, it was settled. This was between me and God.

My husband and I kept loving him and praying for his return. After being so beaten up by the life he fell back into, Jake eventually made his way back to the Lord. He returned to God and to our home. He hadn't quite yet returned to me. We still had a long road ahead of us.

Step-parenting is a challenging call. It will require a lot of sacrifice. It is important that a stepmom/dad have a clear understanding of what they are signing up for.

Blending a family can be downright difficult. There will be hurdles to leap and nothing is easy about it. In fact, it can be extremely painful at times. But you must keep at it. Though it may hurt you to the core, the best thing a stepparent can do is to hold on tightly to their faith and ask God for the grace to get through it all. He is more than able.

We can't reject because we are rejected. It was this same type of love God gave to us who rejected Him. He chose us and chooses us again and again. And this love that we receive, He requires that we give to others. He loves us in spite of ourselves.

A child may tell you (the stepparent) you are not their parent. They may think if they reject this new arrangement it will go away or take some power away from you. They may refuse your display of love and affection. That is to be expected. Don't take it to heart. Your child is hurting in some way and can sometimes feel that you are the cause of their pain. Respond with love and wisdom. God tells us to love others the way He loves us. That's pretty profound. John 13:34 says a new commandment I give you, that ye love one another, as I have loved you, that ye also love one another. If we search out God's love, we can get how we are to love these little people who have come into our lives. We were made for love. And chosen to love these precious souls.

Look to the Lord for the right actions and the right words. The scripture reminds us, "A word spoken in due season, how good it is."

If your child belongs to God, then you have to trust the process. Do not try to compensate by spoiling them. It is unhealthy parenting. A biological parent may attempt to offer expensive toys, lavish vacations and the such to make up for their position. This does not make up for it, in fact, it creates the opposite situation in making children feel ill at ease. Children tend to feel insecure when there is no structure, stability and discipline in their lives. It is likely to send the message that the parent does not care. Children need boundaries. The scripture tells us he that loves his child, disciplines him. But he that hates his child does not discipline him (Proverbs 13:24 paraphrased).

God is ultimately in charge of our children's lives.. This doesn't mean they escape disheartening situations. Quite the contrary, we will all suffer in this earth. It's good for us. Trouble makes us stronger. God uses all of it to bring forth His purpose.

Moses was raised in Pharaoh's house on purpose. His biological mother was denied the privilege of rearing him. It was part of his spiritual destiny. He would need to learn Egyptian customs and language to approach Pharaoh. This Egyptian-bred Hebrew would lead God's people into freedom.

Joseph's half-brothers sold him into slavery. Most of these were brothers with whom he shared the same father, but not the same mother. Joseph was thrown in a pit, sold into slavery, falsely accused, and thrown into prison unjustly....on his way to destiny.

So don't feel sorry for your child because he/she has a stepfamily. Your child is among many great men and women. It may not be the ideal situation in our minds. However God always has a plan to turn what the enemy means for evil into something wonderful, all for His glory.

As a stepparent, it's important to remember that your stepchild also belongs to the one you vowed to love. You have to consider how your relationship with the child affects your spouse. If your relationship to the child is estranged, it's going to make things really complicated for your spouse. Love your spouse enough to put in the extra effort. Don't just consider your position. Look at the situation from all perspectives. Blending a family is tough for everybody. But it is possible. And for those who forge through to the other side, there are beautiful rewards.

6
YOURS, MINE, & OURS

From the very beginning of our relationship, when I knew my husband had a son, I knew and accepted that his son would be a part of my life. He was always included in the number of children I had, when answering those who inquired. The math would make me appear to having a baby too soon, still I never explained it. He was not my stepson, but my son. They all were equally *our* children. For me, it was more important to be inclusive of my son than to spare my reputation. It does something for a child when you take that type of stance, defending their right to be in your family.

When people ask how many children we have, we don't break it up or divide it into his children and my children. They are all ours. We love completely. We don't owe others more than we owe our children. So we don't have to break it down. My husband and I are one. We have five children. It's not necessary to say what the biological components are. That's too much (unnecessary) information. Spiritually and emotionally, his son is my son.

In the same way, you owe no explanation to those outside of your family. Let them think whatever they choose.

Rejection is always knocking at the door of the child's heart. A child needs the peace, security and acceptance that they belong. When you separate them, it says they aren't fully yours. To say, "That's Oscar's son or my stepson", even though it's technically fact, it's not truth for me. "Step" puts some distance and space between us. It makes us unofficial. As I said before, I never wanted Jake to feel rejected or less than. He is mine and I am his -fully and forever. That is true no matter what.

As stepparents, our love for the other children God adds to our lives must be unconditional and authentic. If my love is real, than I am his "real" mother.

I, Crystal, also expect my extended family to give Jake the same love and acceptance that is given to the other children. He is a grandson, nephew, cousin and great-grandson. We expect him to be included in family events, photographs, gift-giving, etc. We don't allow anyone to make a difference in our children. My family has been wonderful in this area.

If you are the stepparent, you will have to ensure that your extended family doesn't try to separate your children. They should accept all of the children, justly. Certainly, you can't force them to do so. However you can draw the line in the sand as to what behavior you will tolerate. This also goes for the biological family. The biological parent will have to make sure that that their extended family is not giving preference to the biological child in a way that makes the other children feel disconnected. Let's just love everybody. That's what God intended. We were born to love.

When planning family vacations, it is best to include all the children. It is especially important to invite the noncustodial child(ren) even if they choose not to participate. Don't assume they won't want to go. They should always have the option, even if they have said no a million times before. Ask again. Let it be their choice. You don't want the time that you didn't ask, to be the time they really wanted to come.

Our will and life insurances also reflect what is in our hearts. Our five children are equal beneficiaries. They will each have an equivalent portion in what we bequeath to them. Jake will not receive a lesser portion than the others. He is not a lesser child. In Christ, we have been adopted into the family of God. But we still have a full inheritance.

This is important because at times this is where blended families break down. When one parent dies, the biological or stepchildren are left out of the inheritance. All of your children should receive the inheritance not just those that are "yours" biologically. It stings when that happens. How we divide our money and possessions tell what we really feel. According to the Word of God, our treasure and our heart are in the same place. St. Luke 12:24 says *For where your treasure is, there will your heart be also.*

The most successful blended families don't forget to say, thank you. When you parent together, it is important to recognize the successful inputs of your team members.

On the day that our son, Jake graduated from high school, my husband and I bought a card and flowers for Martha. We said thank you for all that she had done and sacrificed as the custodial parent. It was a token of our appreciation. She was overwhelmed. Something so small meant so much. It was much-needed affirmation. From that moment on, she referred to me as Jake's mom and not his stepmom. People were puzzled, because they knew she was his birth mom. But it was a private acceptance from her to me. I understood and accepted it.

Whenever possible, recognize the labor of the custodial parent. Give affirmation whenever you can. There is a greater labor on the custodial parent. Support and encourage her or him, especially if he or she is single. If you share custody, you should still say thanks and show appreciation. It is totally appropriate to recognize them on Mother's Day and Father's Day. It would also be a good idea to remind your children to honor his/her parent's birthday. Little deposits add up and make blending easier.

7
PETITION

If we are going to have any success in this blending, we must start with our hearts in the right place. You can have the best intentions, but if you are caught up in your emotions, those intentions will fail. You have got to commit to this. Put your flesh under subjection and choose what is right regardless to the days that you are in your feelings. And there will be plenty of those.

Emotions vacillate. We can't build anything upon them. Truth is constant and we can build entire empires and cities on truth. You are embarking on a big challenge – blending a family into one unit. So hold on to truth, no matter what you feel. The way to overcome and win is by asking God for His help.

People will aggravate, irritate, and provoke you. If you respond every time you will be no better than them. Remember this is not just about you. Keep sight of the bigger picture. Choose what is best for your family. You don't have to engage every argument that you are invited to. Ignore pettiness. Learn how to hold your tongue.

Proverbs 17:28 KJV says, even a fool, when he holdeth his peace, is counted wise: and he that shutteth his lips is esteemed a man of understanding. Yes, it is easier said than done. It will require that you stack the odds in your favor by calling on the Lord to help you make right choices when you don't want to. Paul said in his writings that there was a law at work. Romans 7:21 I find then a law, that, when I would do good, evil is present with me. The struggle is real. It takes the work of the Holy Spirit to exercise maturity and prudence in the midst of foolishness.

It will take wisdom to navigate the ground of blending families. The way to wisdom is through prayer. If we ask God, He will answer us. He gives wisdom liberally to those who ask (James 1:5). And Proverbs 16:20 KJV says, He that handleth a matter wisely shall find good: and whoso trusteth in the LORD, happy is he.

My wife and I came to an authentic relationship with the Lord within the first year of our marriage. It was this close connection to God that kept our life on track. We lived our faith out loud, both privately and publically. Our relationship with the Lord greatly influenced my son's mother. The Lord started tugging at her heart and she began to call us to ask questions. We spent hours at a time on the phone. Together, my wife and I prayed with her and for her. We counselled her. She finally submitted her life to God's leading. It was amazing. Of course, this caused us to grow even closer as a parenting team. What a blessing for our little baby boy that all of his parents would walk with the Lord!

If she were alive today, all of us would be speaking on this important subject. She was ordained as a minister before she left the earth. Alas, she is not here, but her son is. He gets to do what she dreamed of doing. Jake is a pastor, preaching and declaring God's word. Growing up, he was surrounded by a wall of prayer. His three parents all prayed for God's plan to come forth in his life.

We were co-laborers in this work to bring this preacher forth. We agreed with God and the result is this extraordinary man who loves his God, his wife, and his five children. He also loves his dad and his mama (me). He walks in integrity. He gives generously to help others. He lives the Word that he preaches. Martha would be smiling.

I know God is.

There are times that relationships between couples don't work out. When that happens, don't let the children get caught in the crossfire. Let God extract glory out of it. He is great at making miracles out of messes.

What is the work that you are called to do? It's the same work that we all are called to do – love. Love even after a rocky relationship. God wants us to always represent Him in every situation possible. If we love people, then we ought to pray for those people we claim to love. What if you are the one that God is choosing to pray for the salvation of your ex? What if God wants to use you and your new family to lead him/her into the kingdom? Accept the charge to pray for every person who directly affects your children. Or perhaps you, as the biological mom, are to pray for your ex and his new family? What if it's your life that will draw them in? At the end of the day, we are to love God and others. That includes those "others" who have hurt us.

Pray in faith believing for change to come. Even when things don't look so positive, keep praying. It is the most important facet of healing.

We did not ever imagine having such an amazing

partnership with Martha. But God did. Martha was never that toxic parent. We didn't always agree but she gave her best effort to make the relationship work for her son. She was his first love. Everyone is not as blessed as we were. We understand that. But we serve a God that specializes in unimaginable situations.

Pray for your child's parents or stepparents. Know that the heart of the king is in the Lord's hand. He can turn it as He wills. He can make the impossible possible. Pray in faith believing for their salvation. And pray regularly for their cooperation in raising a godly seed.

My wife's relationship with Jake's mom was very unusual. Both of them were very intentional in making it work. We often see the scuffle for the attention and the affection of the child(ren). Mainly this stems from insecurity. We personally didn't have to experience that because of the two beautiful women in Jake's life. It really is possible for both sets of parents to be on same team. That's what Martha and my wife did. There were times I was amazed at their interaction. I never felt I had to choose between my wife and my child. And no one should have to choose between the other.

My wife was amazing at handling this situation. As a

young woman who came from a broken family herself, she had the foresight to pray. And it was because of that prayer stated in chapter 2, that the Lord put Jake in the heart of my wife. Because of that it changed the way my wife saw my son. It gave Martha a sense of security that my wife wasn't going to mistreat her son or try to replace her. I believe that is the will of God for every family.

8
CHILD SUPPORT

When we think of child support, we think of the financial responsibility and undergirding coming from the noncustodial parent. This is a valid claim, however let's not limit child support to money. Certainly children need financial support from both parents. But a child needs much more than finances to thrive. They need a system of support emotionally, spiritually, mentally and financially. And that support needs to come from the entire village. Child support is unconditional love. It should be offered lavishly and never withheld as a punishment for bad behavior.

Children need affection. Tangibly that may be demonstrated with hugs and kisses. Even if you are not a touchy-feely kind of person. You need to be that for your child. However if the child is not agreeable to that type of display, affection should be offered to a child's comfort level.

Children need time - with both biological parents. It is important that sufficient effort be made to allow the child time alone to spend with the noncustodial parent. A wise stepparent will step aside to allow the child one-on-one time with his biological parent. There is no reason to be threatened by this arrangement. This is good for your spouse and your stepchild. It is also good for your marriage. Competing with your stepchild for the affection and time of your spouse is selfish and immature. Don't just allow the child alone time to bond with his parent, but encourage it. It's healthy. It's also a good way for the stepparent to support the child.

Children need you to be interested. The stepparent should also make efforts to develop his/her own relationship with the child. Call them and talk to them on the phone, even if it's a short call. Make time to take them out to lunch, bowling, to a trampoline park, paint ball, etc. Shared experiences can be a great way to bond together. Take a painting or cooking class together. Sow time into their lives as much as you can. It may feel awkward in the beginning. But if your heart is sincere, it will eventually feel natural.

Show interest in your children's activities. Put them on your calendar. Be present and show up for them. Children yearn for their parents to show up at their sports activities and performances. This support goes a long way in the life of a child. When the step-parent enters the family unit, he/she is usually blamed for absent biological parents. Even if dad usually misses the soccer game before his new wife, when he is married, the new wife is the easy target. All of a sudden, it's her fault. It's not fair, but it's real. So make sure you, as the stepparent, encourage your spouse to be present, even if you can't be there. Make it a real priority for the child's biological parent to be present.

Technology has made so many new advances, there is no reason why a parent cannot keep in contact with his/her noncustodial children. Video chat is a feature available on many phones these days. However Google Hangouts, Skype, Facetime, Marko Polo, are just a few of the many apps that allow you to connect with your child/teen face to face. Parents should connect with their children as often as possible.

Show-up to parent-teacher conferences. Go on field trips. Being physically present shows that you care. A child wants and needs a real relationship with their biological non-custodial parent.

Get to know their friends. Maybe invite a friend along for your time shared. Pay attention to their stories. It may sound redundant, but hear your children. The more that they feel that you are interested and listening, the more they will confide in you.

All children need discipline and correction. You can't play it safe as the noncustodial parent and make the custodial parent the bad guy. Get involved in the discipline. Work together with your child's other parent to make the best decisions for your child. Physical discipline should be weaned as a child gets older. By the time the child is between 11 and 12, it should cease. Parents will have to be creative and take away time and activities to encourage responsible behavior. Grounding a child is far more effective with an older child than physical punishment

It is unwise to sabotage what the stricter parent has set in place. Your child needs you to support the other parent. This can create consistency in the child's life. And you will reap the benefits of that much earlier, when you are on the same page. But if you do not support the other parent, the child will play that to his/her advantage.

A stepparent should ease into this area of support. Wisdom requires stepparents to sit on the sidelines when it comes to discipline. A stepparent has to be eased into the area of correction and discipline. Love and support is what is needed in the beginning.

Children also need money. The biggest financial burden often lies on the custodial parent. If you are the noncustodial parent, understand that in most cases, you are not carrying your full share of the load. Under average circumstances, the financial support awarded by the court is not enough to take care of the child. It is usually not even half the support the child needs. So don't slack in this area.

Don't just give the predetermined amount set by the courts or other. Pick up extra expenses whenever possible. This will require a large sacrifice. Too often, the noncustodial parent looks at his own financial burden to determine what he can contribute to the child. Unfortunately, that is not the complete picture. He also needs to consider the needs of the child and the undue burden left on the custodial parent. If he looks at the whole picture, he can see why what he gives may not be sufficient. Give generously to support your child(ren). It's not the child's fault that your relationship didn't make it. So don't withhold financial support because you are upset with the other parent.

It is your responsibility to take care of your child(ren). Make sure your child has everything she/he needs. Clothing doesn't have to be designer label. However contribute as much as possible.

It is understandable that finances are less ample when you have multiple children to support. However again this is not the child's fault. Ask God for help. And make it work to the best of your ability.

9
OOPS!

Blended or not, families will make mistakes. The adults will trample on each other's feet, sometimes unintentionally and sometimes on purpose. None of us get it all right. We are limited by our humanity.

Heated arguments, refusing to cooperate, gossiping about each other, dirty looks, and foolish nitpicking are standard tools wielded in the step-family dynamic. It can be exhausting. The family unit needs healing to move forward into a better space. And forgiveness is a prerequisite to healing. You all will need to make the choice to let the past be the past. It is not in anyone's best interest to wait on someone else to choose forgiveness, first. Choose it for yourself and for the child(ren).

It is often the case that *everyone* in the village has made missteps. None is innocent. It is important that we start here, acknowledging our own errors because we often get stuck at what was done to us. We are blinded by the injustices of others, we don't take into consideration our own contribution; whether it was a negative tone, harsh response, or even an ungodly thought.

Take the first look at yourself. Could you have handled things differently? Chances are you could have. So stop rehearsing the wounds of the past and decide it's time for a change. Healthy parenting requires that we let go of offenses. When we stop nursing the wounds, they can heal and we can springboard into maturity.

Even if another adult in the village does not choose this high road, you can still improve the relationship by making the choice yourself. The scriptures remind us that we overcome evil with good. Propose a sit-down with all adults on the team. Apologize for your part in the stand-off. Don't worry, if they haven't matured enough to offer an apology to you. Keep showing love. Love is a potent weapon. It is hard to war with someone who is loving you. At some point, they will feel foolish.

Work toward reconciliation. It's necessary. Forgive your ex. That doesn't mean he/she was right. It just means you choose to be righteous by not holding the offense against them. This not only benefits your ex. But it benefits you and your child(ren). When we hold on to unforgiveness and bitterness, we cheat ourselves out of a potentially great relationship and we cheat God out of an astounding testimony. Many testimonies have been blocked because of hardened hearts. Forgiving your ex, their family and/or your ex's new spouse is righteous. It is what God expects from those who are His. Let the good come forth. You can't love God and hate others. God says it's not possible (I John 4:20).

You must choose to forgive for every offense and every repeated offense. Don't allow the past to be present. Move forward, not just for the sake of the children but for your own well-being and healing. It's for your good and for God's glory.

The second part of that is that you will need to apologize to the child(ren). Throughout history, there has been only one perfect parent – God, Himself. The rest of us are subject to error.

Children will be angry and hurt about some of the choices you have made in the past, including the decision made to break the relationship with their parent. It hurts them. The mature and healthy response again is to admit your wrong. Apologize for bad behavior and then you can move forward with your children. Explain to them in age-appropriate terms so that they can comprehend.

Sometimes parents find it challenging to apologize to their children; but it is one of the most impactful things you can do. You gain trust with your children when you are humble enough to say, "I messed up", not just with the relationship with their parent, but also in relating with them. Be sensitive and honest.

Never make promises to your child that you are unable to keep. If there is the slightest chance you may not be able to keep them, don't make it. Kids carry broken promises into adulthood. If you do find yourself in an unavoidable position where you have to break a promise, admit it, apologize for it, and make it up to them (if feasible). Then don't repeat it. It's hard to believe you are sorry for something if you continue to do it. Blaming the other parent or justifying your wrong choices will only make things worse.

Be the example you want your child to emulate. Clear the air. Don't dismiss your child's feelings like they don't matter. When you offend a child, there is an open wound left unattended. It is our duty to nurse their wounds with love and tenderness. Ask for their forgiveness. Pray for their healing. Kids are people, too.

Step-parenting is tough because relating is tough. Make the decision to come alongside your spouse to parent together. What works for one child may not work for another. Children are different. So give yourself some grace. Do what you can. Give your best.

If your child won't forgive you (in that season), just wait them out to the next one. One day, they will see things through more mature eyes. Keep showing the love of God and they will eventually come around. Believe that things can be different. You can have the best relationship possible with your village. It will take lots of love, forgiveness, and patience. But you can have a relationship that glorifies God. It is within reach.

10
BLENDING ADULTS

The hardest families to blend are when the children are already grown. Adult children bring power struggles to the relationship. Parents and children can feel challenged by each other. It becomes a battle of the wills and struggle for control.

The mistake that parents make with adult children is thinking that these adults don't matter in the greater scheme of things. They do matter. They are your family. It is important to not dismiss them.

Parents may also feel that their relationship is none of their child's or spouse's child's business. This is true. Your relationship is yours alone. However, keep in mind that you want a completely healthy blended family. You two are a small part of something bigger. The idea is to be inclusive, not exclusive.

So treat adults like adults. The adult children should

be included when making decisions about the family, not decisions for you two as a couple. Family reunions, gatherings, holidays, and other events should be open to discussion. Your adult children should have a say. Consider their ideas and suggestions. Try to be accommodating when you can.

Adult children will have to figure out and determine where they will fit in the family structure. Be sensitive and understanding. It can be as equally as difficult for an adult child to adjust to a new family as it is for a minor child. In some cases, it's more difficult.

Many times those adults aren't ready for the parent to take on a new love interest and they really don't know how to respond or where they fit. It's unfamiliar territory.

As we've said before, communication is key. Allow a time for adult children to talk about their feelings to their parent without the stepparent present. Let them know that you will listen as long as they are respectful in their communication. That means no name-calling, yelling, offensive tone, or profanity will be tolerated.

Listen and address the concerns of your adult children in a mature fashion. Offer respect and honor to them. Keep their confidence. Everything an adult child shares with their parent should not be shared with the stepparent. The stepparent has to honor their privacy and not demand that his/her spouse share their child's private information with them. Proverbs 16:20a says he that handles a matter wisely findeth good. The wise parent will keep their adult child's confidence. Adult children need to be able to trust their parent with their personal information.   That includes how they may be feeling toward the stepparent. If they ask you not to share something with your spouse, you have a duty to honor that.

Don't attack, demean, or disrespect the adult children's other parent. Remember this new person (stepparent) is your dream, not theirs. So don't try to force it or pretend it's something that it's not. Prayer can change any situation.

Emphasize the importance of all members of your family. Let the adult children know that they are loved and accepted. Don't assume that this is just understood. Adults struggle with rejection, too. Show acceptance.

Don't treat them like outsiders. Make it clear that they are part of the family and are welcome to participate in all activities and events, if they choose. If they choose not to be involved, let that be their decision, too. Continue to pray, show love and be engaged in their life. Sometimes it takes a little while for them to come on board. If you give them enough grace, it can work in your favor.

Don't treat your adult children unjustly. You can't treat everyone the same because people are different and have different needs. But make sure that you are giving proper time, effort, and attention to all. Don't make one child feel lesser than another. If an adult child feels neglected or left out, it will be hard to win them over.

It may feel more uncomfortable and awkward relating with adult stepchildren. However, this only means you and your spouse will have to work past your level of comfort to bring healing to the relationship. Be persistent.

Be reasonable about your expectations. In most cases, an adult child is not looking for a parental relationship. If it happens, great. But if it doesn't, a friendship is just as valuable.

The golden rule applies. Treat them like you want to be treated. Just as the adult children shouldn't interfere in stepparent's relationship with his/her spouse, the stepparent should not interfere in their relationship with their parent. Give them space to have alone time with their parent. This reassures them of their place with their mom or dad. The adult children need to know that their relationship will only get better with you in the picture, not worse.

In reality, there are some adult children with whom there is nothing you can do to make life better. They refuse to allow healing or any one new in their hearts. And there is no part of them that is mature enough to act civil. In those cases, be kind. It may be heart wrenching, but stay the course in prayer. Don't write them off. Continue with the invites, even though they may never attend an event. Always leave room for them to come in. They will never be able to rightly say they weren't welcomed.

Draw clear boundaries about respect. If your adult child cannot respect your spouse, he/she cannot be allowed to disrupt your home. That doesn't mean you can't have a relationship with him/her (you want to win them over). Certainly If they want time with you, offer it to them. Spend time with your son or daughter outside of the home. But they can't be allowed to come into your home if they are bent on disrespecting your spouse.

Your spouse must be priority above your adult

children. No other person comes before your spouse. Present yourselves as a unified team. Let nothing they say or do divide you. Remember you are teaching your adult children how marriage is to be lived out. So keep praying and believing God for them.

The rules for all children should be the same. There should not be a different set of rules for either spouse's children. If you loan money to his children, then the same should apply to her children. (except in a case where an adult child has abused or lost their privileges). If her children are allowed to drive the car, his children should also be allowed.

Sometimes you have to refresh a page to see updated information on a computer. And there are times you need to refresh your family to get everyone on the same page and moving forward. In this case, apologies are in order. Apologize for old offenses, miscommunications, and anything that keeps you from unity. Ask for input on making your family more cohesive. And really consider the input given by the adult children.

Target your prayers for their hearts to be healed from all the pain and damage done in the past. Meet them right where they are. Do what you can.

Pray for the wisdom to navigate the relationship in a way that pleases God. But ultimately you have to leave the results up to Him.

11
ARE WE BLENDED YET?

The ideal situation is to have the two families blend into one seamless unit, loving, sharing life, and laughing together. But what happens when you look at the dream and your reality and the two just don't match up? What do you do when the two families don't feel like one? Maybe the kids are territorial and still create a big divide. They aren't comfortable with the new kids or the new parent in the family.

Cut yourself some slack. Remember that it won't happen in a week or even over a month. It can take years to adjust to each other. Don't put yourself on a timeline or compare yourself to another family. The fact that you are in it and willing to work at it, is a victory in itself.

Count the small wins. For example, a child prays for the stepparents or his stepsiblings for the first time. Or if he wants to spend the night for the first time. Celebrate the small things on your way to the big triumphs. You may not be in the place that you are aiming, but you are making progress.

Hopefully, you have committed to be in the marriage for a lifetime. That means you have time to blend and to create new memories. So don't watch the clock. Be patient with yourself and the other members of your family.

If it's been a number of years, don't count yourself out. Keep going. That's the point of all families, to keep working at it. Healthy families never give up. If you've tried something that just hasn't worked, try something else. And keep trying. At the end of your life, you want to know that you have given your all.

Make sure that you are praying together as a family. Family devotionals are a helpful way to engage your team. Give each of the children an opportunity to lead the devotional time. Make it fun. Do not spend your family devotion time lecturing or preaching to your children. It will turn into another thing that they dread.

Create new traditions as a family. Be very intentional. For example, play games together. However never pit bloodline against bloodline. This will make your bonding much tougher. You could make it girls against boys or kids against the parents. But NEVER set the stepchildren against the biological children. Trouble is inevitable.

You could also host a movie night, once a week. Each child gets an opportunity to choose the movie and everyone has to watch it. (You will probably need some age-appropriate rules about this one – regarding rating and type of movie). Or maybe you could have a karaoke night.

If you share joint custody, you can make the transition smoother for your child(ren). Add something fun. For example, a trip to the Dollar Store or a stop at the convenience store to get a favorite drink each time you pick up the kids from the other parent's house. This helps to lighten the anxiety and helps the kids adjust.

Remember to celebrate holidays and birthdays. If the custodial parent hosts a birthday party for your child, make it a priority. If for some reason you are unable to make it, choose the day before or after to celebrate your child. Let them know ahead of time that you won't make it so that they won't be disappointed from expecting you. Make these important bonding times for your children. It hurts a child (adult or minor) when their parent doesn't acknowledge their birthday. Do something. It doesn't have to be big or expensive. It just has to be done. Celebrate holidays with your child. The day after Thanksgiving or Christmas Eve. Make your own memories with your noncustodial children.

Don't sweat the small stuff. Overlook small infractions for the greater good of the relationship. Every battle does not need to be fought. If you are building a family, forgiveness will have to be a staple. Be willing to let the small things go.

The disruption of a family, regardless to the circumstances surround it, is traumatic. And those affected by the trauma will need the proper tools and time to heal. Allow children the opportunity to sort things out. Sometimes you will have to talk them through it. They may not have considered something that seems obvious to you. You will need loads of patience. If necessary, seek therapy. Some children experience depression, anxiety or may act out in other ways. Therapy may be the help you need to get to that healthy place. Bringing in a pair of professional and objective eyes, can be beneficial to all the family members.

Regardless to where you are in the process, a blended family is still a family. You will have all the dynamics of any other family. There absolutely will be misunderstandings, disagreements, and family squabbles. You will have to sort through it all. But know that these are not unique to your family. Every family on the earth has some kind of issue.

The key is to keep praying, learning, and growing. Your family will eventually become more close knit than where they started. Celebrate every victory and every step taken closer toward togetherness, no matter how small. Give honor to God who is the repairer of the breach. And Happy blending!

ABOUT THE AUTHORS

Oscar & Crystal Jones have been married more than 37 years. The two are cofounders of Marriage For A Lifetime Ministries a 501C3 nonprofit organization. They teach and advocate for strong healthy marriages. The couple have 7 children and 9 amazing grandchildren who are the joy of their lives. They have authored and co-authored several books.

Other Books by the Authors

Church Unusual

Extreme Money Makeover

Fast Food for the Married Soul

Hot Dates for Married Lovers

Naked Sex

Ring Talks

The Newlywed Handbook

The S Word : What Submission Is Not

When The Vow Breaks

...and many others

www.ingramcontent.com/pod-product-compliance
Lightning Source LLC
LaVergne TN
LVHW011337080426
835513LV00006B/410